S0-DZD-014

SINGER'S CHRISTIAN WEDDING COLLECTION

ISBN 0-7935-9368-9

HAL•LEONARD®
CORPORATION

7777 W. BLUEMOUND RD. P.O. BOX 13819 MILWAUKEE, WI 53213

Visit Hal Leonard Online at
www.halleonard.com

SINGER'S CHRISTIAN WEDDING COLLECTION

Butterfly Kisses

Recorded by Bob Carlisle

Words and Music by RANDY THOMAS
and BOB CARLISLE

Bbsus2   Csus   C   Bbsus2/D   Csus2/E   F(add2)   Bbsus2/D

I close my eyes   and I thank God _ for all _   of the joy   in   my _ life,
rib - bons and curls.   Try-ing her wings _ out   in a great   big   world, _
said, "I'm not sure,   I just feel like _ I'm los - ing my ba - by   girl." _

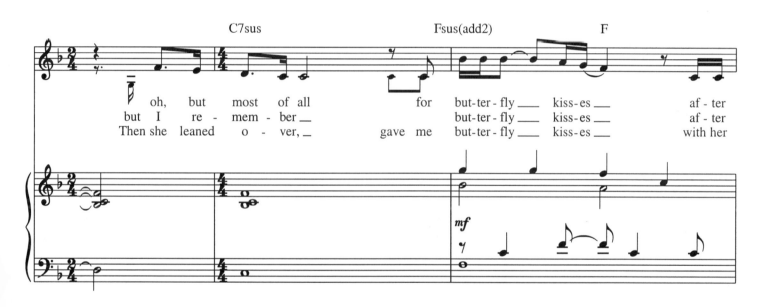

C7sus   Fsus(add2)   F

oh, but   most   of all   for   but-ter-fly _ kiss-es _   af - ter
but I re - mem - ber _   but-ter-fly _ kiss-es _   af - ter
Then she leaned o - ver, _   gave me   but-ter-fly _ kiss-es _   with her

mf

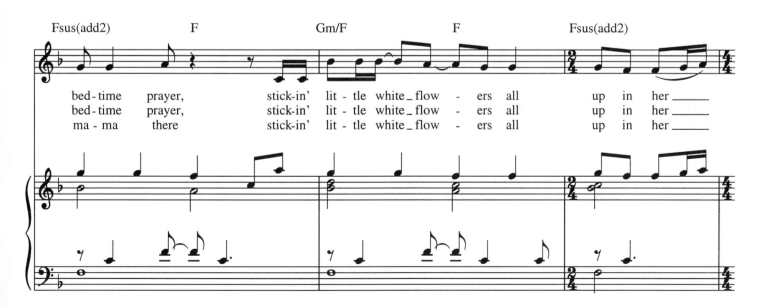

Fsus(add2)   F   Gm/F   F   Fsus(add2)

bed - time   prayer,   stick-in' lit - tle white _ flow - ers all   up in her _____
bed - time   prayer,   stick-in' lit - tle white _ flow - ers all   up in her _____
ma - ma   there   stick-in' lit - tle white _ flow - ers all   up in her _____

6

CODA

Cherish the Treasure

Recorded by Steve Green

Words and Music by
JON MOHR

Commitment Song
Recorded by Chris & Diane Machen

Words and Music by ROBERT STERLING
and CHRIS MACHEN

O Lord,_ dear Lord, we come be-fore_ You now_ to
O Lord,_ dear Lord, let us nev-er turn_ a - way._ Let us

of - fer You_ a sac - ri - fice_ of praise._ And we pray, dear_ Lord, You'll
hon - or You_ and al - ways seek_ Your face._ And we pray, dear_ Lord, for -

bless our sol - emn vow___ that as long as we're_ to - geth - er___ the name of
give us when_ we stray._ Lead us back with ten - der mer - cy___ with Your

Flesh of My Flesh

Recorded by Leon Patillo

Words and Music by
LEON PATILLO

For Always

Recorded by BeBe & CeCe Winans

Words and Music by BEBE WINANS,
BILLY SPRAGUE and KEITH THOMAS

Slowly, with expression

27

Go There with You

Recorded by Steven Curtis Chapman

Words and Music by
STEVEN CURTIS CHAPMAN

Love of the Lasting Kind

Words and Music by CLAIRE CLONINGER
and DON CASON

God Causes All Things to Grow

Recorded by Steve Green

Words and Music by STEVEN CURTIS CHAPMAN
and STEVE GREEN

Household of Faith

Recorded by Steve & Marijean Green

Words by BRENT LAMB
Music by JOHN ROSASCO

With warmth (= 66)

Here we are __ at the start __ com-mit-ting to __ each
oth-er by His Word and from our hearts. We will be __ a fam-i-ly __
__ in a house that will __ be a home, and with faith we'll build it strong. We'll build a

How Beautiful

Recorded by Twila Paris

Words and Music by
TWILA PARIS

53

54

55

57

I Could Never Promise You

Words and Music by
DON FRANCISCO

I could nev - er prom - ise _ you on just my strength a - lone, _

that all my life I'd care for _ you and love you as my own.

I've nev - er known the fu - ture, I on - ly see to - day; _

ter - ni - ty ___ goes by, the life and love He's giv-en us ___

are nev - er going to die. ___

are nev - er going to die. ___

The life and love He's giv-en us ___ are nev-er going to die.

I Will Be Here

Recorded by Steven Curtis Chapman

Words and Music by
STEVEN CURTIS CHAPMAN

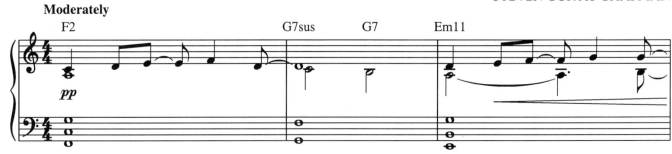

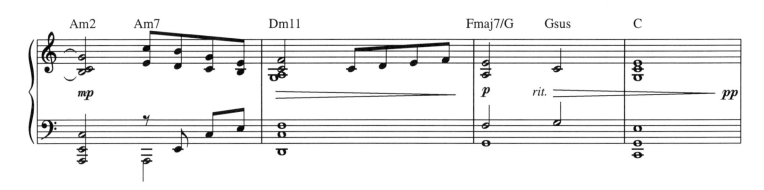

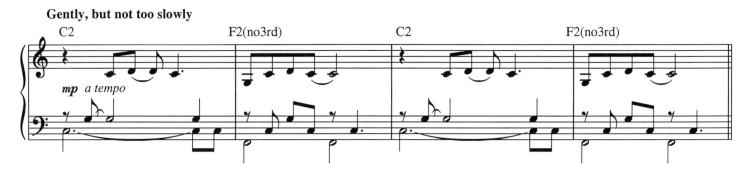

To-mor-row morn-in' if you ___ wake up and the sun does ___ not ___ ap-pear, ___

To-mor-row morn-in' if you ___ wake up and the fu-ture is ___ un-clear, ___

64

In This Very Room

Words and Music by RON and CAROL HARRIS

I.O.U. Me
Recorded by BeBe & CeCe Winans

Words and Music by BEBE WINANS, BILLY SPRAGUE,
KEITH THOMAS, THOMAS HEMBY and MIKE RAPP

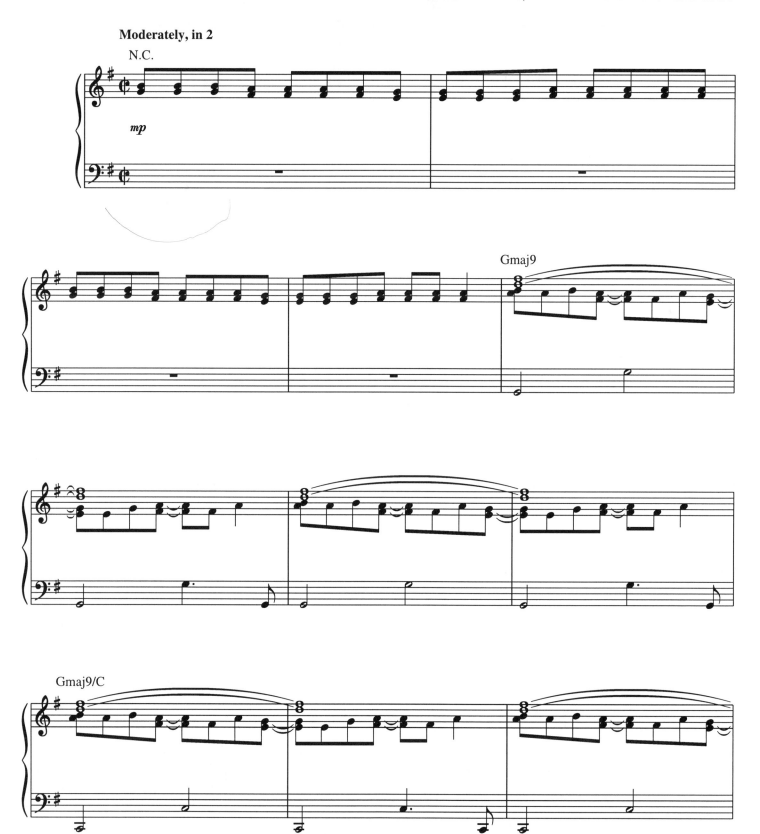

When I saw ___ ___ you, ___ me ___

I could see ___ that it ___ was me ___
it was true ___ what you ___ went through, ___

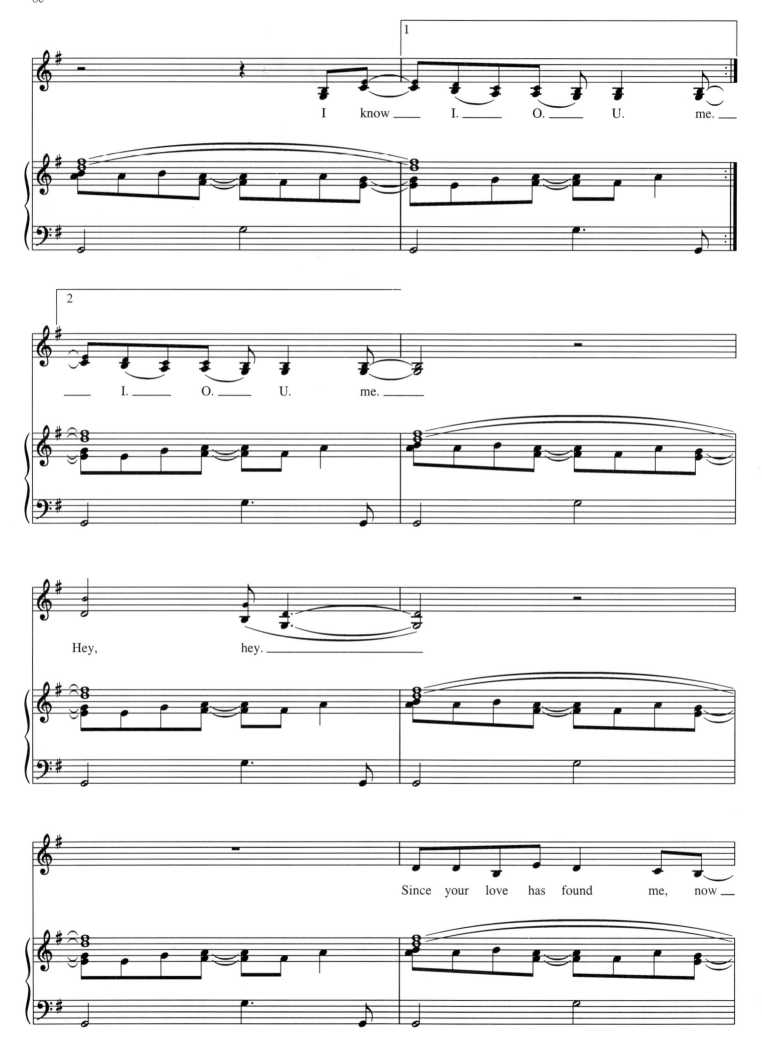

The Language of Jesus Is Love

Recorded by Scott Wesley Brown

Words and Music by PHILL McHUGH, GREG NELSON,
SCOTT WESLEY BROWN and PHIL NAISH

Moderately slow, with expression

84

The Lord's Prayer

By ALBERT HAY MALOTTE

Poco meno mosso, e sonoramente

liv - er us from e - vil: For thine is the king - dom, _____ and the pow - er, _____ and the glo - ry, _____ for - ev - er. _____ A - men. _____

Tempo I°

rallentando e morendo

Lost Without You
Recorded by BeBe & CeCe Winans

Words and Music by BEBE WINANS
and KEITH THOMAS

Love Will Be Our Home
Recorded by Sandi Patty

Words and Music by
STEVEN CURTIS CHAPMAN

The ending either could be done loud or soft.

Only God Could Love You More

Words and Music by DWIGHT LILES
and NILES BOROP

Moderately fast, tenderly

I asked the Lord _ for some - one, _ and I al - ways knew _
I'm tempt-ed to _ be say - ing _ that we met _ by chance, _

that in God's time and in God's way _ it would
but God was there at ev - 'ry turn, _ in

be some-one like you. _____ All my hopes and
ev - 'ry cir-cum - stance. _____ To share this life God

Parent's Prayer
(Let Go of Two)
Recorded by Steven Curtis Chapman

Words and Music by
GREG DAVIS

Moderately, with emotion

Song of Reconciliation

Recorded by Susan Ashton, Margaret Becker & Christine Denté

Words and Music by
WAYNE KIRKPATRICK

110

Perfect Union

Words and Music by JOHN ANDREW SCHREINER
and MATTHEW WARD

Portrait of Love

Recorded by John Byron

Words and Music by KENNY WOOD
and BILLY CROCKETT

Flowing, not too slow

He would-n't sit still long e-nough to
trav-el-in' art-ist known as Paul

have his por-trait done. His heart was set to
paint-ed truth with words. The truth that he spoke was

move his life at twice the speed of love. An
burn-ing love that com-forts and dis-turbs.

Seekers of Your Heart

Words and Music by MELODIE TUNNEY,
DICK TUNNEY and BEVERLY DARNALL

126

This Is the Day
(A Wedding Song)

Words and Music by
SCOTT WESLEY BROWN

This Very Day

Recorded by Paul Overstreet

Words and Music by JOHN ELLIOTT
and PAUL OVERSTREET

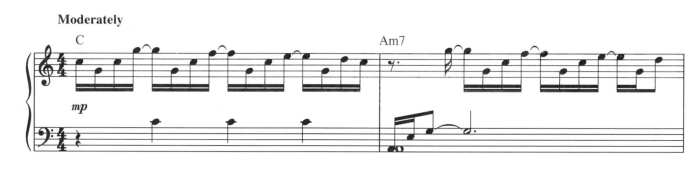

I've been search-ing all ___ my life ___ for the
Like the an-swer to ___ my prayers, ___ from

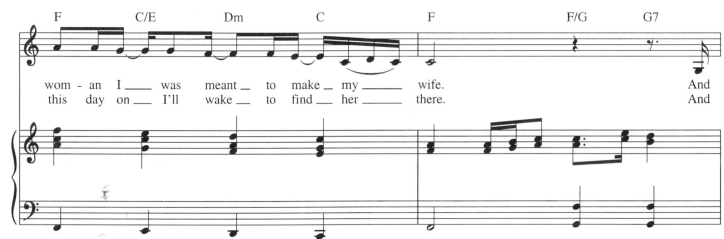

wom-an I ___ was meant ___ to make ___ my ___ wife. And
this day on ___ I'll wake ___ to find ___ her ___ there. And

The Wedding

Recorded by Michael Card

Words and Music by
MICHAEL CARD

Moderately, with a lilt

Lord of Light, oh come to this wed-ding; take the doubt and dark-ness a-way.

CODA

Time for Joy

Recorded by Lawrence Craig Shackley

Words and Music by
GERRY LIMPIC

Moderately slow, with expression

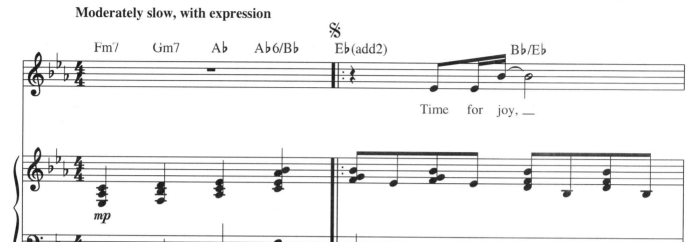

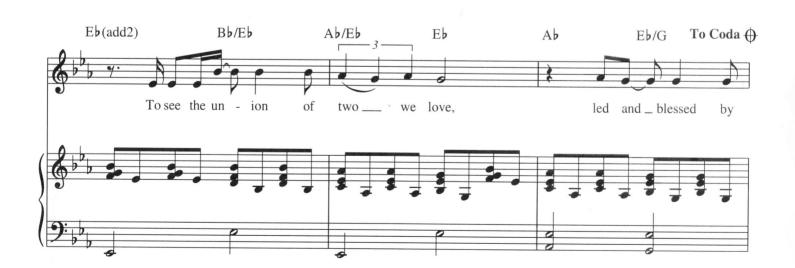

142

D.S. al Coda

Wedding Prayer

Words and Music by
MARY RICE HOPKINS

Gently in four ♩ = 82

Lord, _____ take our lives _____ As two who love You _____ join as one.
Fa - ther, _____ You are love _____ From the be - gin - ning of time. _____
Lord, _____ use our lives _____ As we jour - ney from year. _____

And let our love grow _____ as Your love _____
You made us to join _____ as
And make our love strong _____ yet,

_____ grows in us, _____ Bind us to - geth - er so we
man and _____ wife, _____ To live to - geth - er, the Cre -
gen - tle and true, _____ In all that we are _____ let us

Where There Is Love
Recorded by Scott Wesley Brown

Words and Music by PHILL McHUGH
and GREG NELSON

Where there is love, the bruised can find a re-fuge to be held close un-til their tears are gone. Where there is love the wea-ry can re-vive their hope un-til they're

Wedding
COLLECTIONS FOR VOICE
From Hal Leonard

THE SINGER'S WEDDING ANTHOLOGY

An unprecedented, comprehensive look at wedding repertoire. Rather than just one style of music, like most wedding collections for voice, we have included classical and traditional material, popular songs, and contemporary Christian music. The anthology is available in 3 versions: High Voice, Low Voice, and Duets. The two solo volumes (High and Low) contain the same 45 selections, but in appropriate keys to high or low voices. Includes: I Swear • Just the Way You Are • When I Fall in Love • Someone Like You • The Language of Jesus Is Love • God Causes All Things to Grow • I Will Be Here • Ave Maria • Bist Du Bei Mir • Entreat Me Not to Leave Thee • Panis Angelicus • Whither Thou Goest • and many others. The duet collection contains 25 songs, including: Up Where We Belong • All I Ask of You • Endless Love • Let It Be Me • Household of Faith • Jesu Joy of Man's Desiring • Panis Angelicus • and many others.

00740006	High Voice	$19.95
00740008	Low Voice	$19.95
00740005	Duets	$14.95

WEDDING CLASSICS

The definitive collection of 12 classical and traditional favorites for the wedding service, packaged with an excellent recording of full performances (featuring top quality young singers) and accompaniments only. Contents: Bist du Bei Mir (Bach) • Entreat Me Not to Leave Thee (Gounod) • Because, Wher'er You Walk (Handel) • Oh Promise Me, Ich Liebe Dich (Grieg) • Ave Maria (Schubert) • Ave Maria (Bach/Gounod) • Du Ring An Meinem Finger (Schumann) • Widmung (Schumann) • I Love You Truly, Pur Ti Miro (Monteverdi – duet).

00740053	High Voice Book/CD package	$17.95
00740054	Low Voice Book/CD package	$17.95

10 POPULAR WEDDING DUETS

with a companion CD

10 duets for the wedding. The companion CD contains two performances of each song, one with singers, the other is the orchestrated instrumental track for accompaniment. Contents: All I Ask of You • Annie's Song • Don't Know Much • Endless Love • I Swear • In My Life • Let It Be Me • True Love • Up Where We Belong • When I Fall in Love.

00740002	Book/CD package	$19.95

10 WEDDING SOLOS

with a companion CD

A terrific, useful collection of 10 songs for the wedding, including both popular songs and contemporary Christian material. There are two versions of each song on the companion CD, first with full performances with singers, then with the instrumental accompaniments only. Contents: Here, There and Everywhere • I Swear • The Promise • Someone Like You • Starting Here Starting Now • God Causes All Things to Grow • Parent's Prayer • This Is the Day • Wedding Prayer • Where There Is Love.

00740004	High Voice Book/CD package	$19.95
00740009	Low Voice Book/CD package	$19.95

12 WEDDING SONGS

arranged for medium voice and fingerstyle guitar

A practical collection of music chosen particularly for the wedding, in new arrangements designed to flatter voice with guitar accompaniment. The collection combines classical/traditional and popular selections. The guitar part is presented in both standard notation and tablature. Contents: Annie's Song • Ave Maria (Schubert) • The First Time Ever I Saw Your Face • Here, There and Everywhere • I Swear • If • In My Life • Jesu, Joy of Man's Desiring • Let It Be Me • Unchained Melody • When I Fall in Love • You Needed Me.

00740007		$12.95

SINGER'S CHRISTIAN WEDDING COLLECTION

30 songs, including: Butterfly Kisses • Cherish the Treasure • Commitment Song • Household of Faith • How Beautiful • I Will Be Here • Lost Without You • Love Will Be Our Home • Parent's Prayer (Let Go of Two) • This Is the Day (A Wedding Song) • and more.

00740108	High Voice	$19.95
00740109	Low Voice	$19.95

FOR MORE INFORMATION, SEE YOUR LOCAL MUSIC DEALER, OR WRITE TO:

HAL•LEONARD® CORPORATION

7777 W. BLUEMOUND RD. P.O. BOX 13819 MILWAUKEE, WI 53213

Prices, contents and availability subject to change without notice. Some products may not be available outside the U.S.A.